Grow
Growi
Growing in to me

Sammy Barcroft

Growing up… Growing old… Growing in to me © 2022 Sammy Barcroft

All rights reserved.

No part of this publication may be reproduced, stored in a retrieval system, or transmitted, in any form or by any means, electronic, mechanical, photocopying, recording or otherwise, without the prior written permission of the presenters.

Sammy Barcroft asserts the moral right to be identified as author of this work.

Presentation by *BookLeaf Publishing*

Web: www.bookleafpub.com

E-mail: info@bookleafpub.com

ISBN: 9789357695428

First edition 2022

ACKNOWLEDGEMENT

My moon sister Jeannie for always giving me the shove I need! My husband and family for always believing in me and loving me endlessly. My best friends for being my biggest cheerleaders.

PREFACE

Having always enjoyed writing but never really knowing where to start, this seemed like the perfect challenge. Poetry, blogs, articles, journals - writing has always been a big part of my life. Sometimes our fear gets in the way of us moving any further towards our goals, so removing those barriers and breaking the goal down into achievable chunks illuminates our path.

Your path

Being different.
A curse or a privilege?
Being the same.
Vulgarity or a dream?
Walking your own path is a freedom, a liberty
An invocation of your true self.
Finding that path can feel like a chore. But it's always worth it.
Choose yourself. Always

Darkness

It's a place we visit sometimes, isn't it.
Darkness.

Does it suffocate you? Restrictive,
uncomfortable, unmoving. The weight, the
colour, the confinement, the intensity.
Or Does it set you free? Enveloping you in the
velvet softness, silent, strong, familiar.

It's a place I visit.
Darkness.

Being hugged tight in the constraints of
darkness, melting into the blackness of the night,
absorbing the lower vibrations and having
permission to close your eyes. Feeling so
constricted, you're breathless. Feeling the vice
like grip around your heart. Memories slipping
away into nothing. Mind clearing. Black.

Softness, silent, still, velvet, smooth. Relaxing
back into the comfy winged armchair. Being
covered with a weighted blanket, sinking deeper
into the bouncy mattress. Mind clearing.
Meditative. Black.

It's not always a bad place to visit.

Take comfort in the darkness, for black contains all the colours.

You must

When you know what you have to do….

But you don't want to.
But it's scary.
But you don't know the outcome.
But you can't quite surrender.
But you don't want to unearth all that trauma.
But you don't want to relive it.

But you know you must ♥

Woman.

Empowered.
Free.
Fire.
Confidence.
Goddess.
Within.
Choice.
Beautiful.
Yes.
Focus.
Natural.
Warrior.
Power.
Liberated.
Woman.

Water

The swirling of the water.
The kiss of the air.
The touch of the cold.
The shiver of the nerves.
The fascination of the action.
The release of emotion.
The realisation of empowerment.
The thrill of the achievement.
The magic of the memories.
The exhilaration.
The depth.
The dark.
The water

Other peoples opinions

Don't let anyone dull your sparkle.

Don't believe anyone else's narrative about you.

Don't ever believe you aren't worthy or you can't do it.

The future is yours for the taking, the present is a gift - now to enjoy, the past has taught us lessons
and how to move forward.

Timely reminder

There is nothing like hearing devastating news to make you consider your own mortality. I love my life, I love the fact I'm ageing - it really is a privilege afforded to so few.

I'm reminded of that.

Go live your life, look after your body, your mind, your loves. Move forward with no regrets. Forgive much, release everything, always be gracious and grateful.

Be brave, be bold, grab everything with two hands. Ask for help, talk, laugh, sing, dance.

You deserve happiness.

Fun

Can we talk about fun?

Can you remember the last time you had fun?
Can you remember when your inner child totally giggled and tickled your sides? When you unashamedly let go and just went with it? -
When you laughed from your soul and your eyes lit up?

It's good for the mind, body and soul y'know. I urge you to get out there and have some fun as soon as humanly possible.
Life is so serious and scary.
you may have a serious or very sensible job, nothing may seem much fun - I know, I know.

But babe, I'm here to tell you this - life is more fun when you're laughing.
Life is easier when you slot in some play.
Life is more fulfilling when you give in to that inner child
and just have some fun.

Not so Mum tum

The 'Not so Mum Tum'

Pictures of me, fat tummy and all. I won't lie - it took a while to love them. When I first saw them, my resolve to lose weight and tone up was at the forefront of my mind.

Then I got a grip...
Is my tummy something to be ashamed of? No
Is it something I could do something about? I could
Is it something I'm going to torture myself with? No, I'm not. This is how I look
Is it something I'm going to punish myself to reduce in size? No, definitely not. No change ever began with hate.

But it does make me think about fat tummies and how society views them.

If I were a mum, I would possibly hear all the praise... you grew and birthed a baby. Stretch marks are tiger stripes of honour. Your tummy housed life. It deserves to look like that, isn't it amazing. And this is so so true, I'm not taking away from this at all. If you are a mumma, I'm 100% your biggest supporter. You are epic and you should be so proud.

But there's a little voice inside me that says - that's not me. That's not something I can feel proud of and it's right to an extent. No babies here. I guess sometimes that equals in my mind - No excuse to look like I do.

This isn't a pity party, that I haven't had children or even that I'm fat - I'm cool with both. But it's a thought about the narrative we speak and the language we use.

Should I be excluded of being proud of my tummy as it hasn't birthed children. No of course not. But What can I be proud of my tummy for? Well I'm proud of my tummy as it's part of my body that keeps me alive & keeps me going for starters.

Women supporting women, regardless of any characteristics.

So go celebrate mum tums, not so mum tums and everything in between. Please go be proud, wear the bikini, wear the nice lingerie.

You are a woman and you are amazing. I promise you, whatever you size, ability, colour, creed - you are AMAZING.

Dieting

For as long as I can remember I've been on a diet - ones I've made up, I've been sold, ones I've punished myself with. Through those years, all thats happened is I've got fatter & my eating has become more erratic & disordered.

I was told when I was about 7 yrs old - I was too fat to do a handstand, by a family member. I was then shamed with the fit of clothes, shamed around food & shamed for existing. Lets be clear, I was a child, I wasn't fat, I wasn't even a chubby child, even if I had been, this was not ok.

I'm lucky enough now to know this is a trigger. I know what a binge cycle looks like, know how to address this (yes theres work to do) I know this is self destruct and this isn't motivation. Being kind and loving myself is.

I used to truly believe being thin would make life better, it would be the miracle cure for EVERYTHING. I don't think that anymore. I know now my weight doesn't equal my worth. It's taken a long time. But I know the feels.

This is why people making money out of the misery of others is currently making me mad. Social media is full of ads for herbal life, juice+, some other shit. People using it, promoting it, actively selling it as the answer to your prayers. Selling it as the easy option. Disguising it as well-being.

It frightens me to death that people buy this shit, hoping for a better life. Parting with money they don't have, to buy the products for their use and then try and sell them alongside their diet. The failure is too hard to contemplate. Hell the success is hard to comtemplate. What happens when you're a size 8, your mental health is shit and life is still crap, then what?

I see these adds and feel that familial pull, I could do that, lose weight quick. Even the thought of it and what it entails sends me straight into a biscuit hole. Food as punishment. That's not life.

Don't get me wrong - if it's for you fill your boots. But be careful, please be kind and considerate with your ads. There may be people who aren't as strong as I am watching. We are not failures being fat. You have no idea who we are. And we can do fucking handstands.

So
Here I am... turning my back on diet culture.

Diets can fuck right off. Nothing in a diet is healthy. Shakes, pills, tea, meal replacements, even surgery... none of it fixes your brain. None of it fixes you.

We need to do the work, do the therapy, undo all the damage diet culture has forced upon us, before focusing on our issues. Losing weight isn't the answer to 99.9% of our problems or issues. They will still be there, we'll just be fitting in smaller clothes/places with the same issues.

Nourish your body, move it occasionally, treat it well, talk to it kindly. I think you'll find it just wants to be your friend. Listen to it let out a sigh of relief when you choose understanding and compassion and change your motivation.

No one else is the enemy. Putting others down because of their body shape to make you feel better is shitty too. Come on, we're better than this!

Delete social media accounts who make you feel bad about your body, it's your social media feed

- you curate it. If this shit triggers you, ditch it. And be aware it may trigger others too - eating disorders are much more common than you'd ever believe.

When you talk unkindly to and about yourself, think of those around you listening, including small people who are forming their own opinions of their own bodies. Words are spells, what we say - we become.

No celebrity got thin quick, no one had a month of shakes and lost all their issues, please remember that. You do not need this negativity in your life, I promise.

If you want to be healthy, to nourish your body, to become stronger, to eat well for yourself and maybe even symptoms of diagnosed medical conditions - honestly I'm your biggest cheerleader. But please don't try and sell me pills, don't line the pockets of fuckwits who know nothing about nutrition, don't buy in to get thin/get rich schemes. Look after you, and those around you, seek proper nutritional wellness help and listen to your body.

Love yourself first and foremost.

Grandmother Moon

I've always loved you from afar, watching your
journey across the night sky. Seeing you appear
in the dark, perpetually showing your glow.
I knew there was magic in the air, the clouds
concealing your beauty. Controlling our tides
with your power and keeping us in line with
your passion.

I stand under the full moon at night and make
my peace with my past. I release the tension,
that what doesn't serve me and am cleansed of
any anger with my tears. I forgive myself, I
forgive others, I forgive. I am cleansed

The ebb and flow, the wax and wane, the full
and new, the cycle is endless. The light, the
dark. The beautiful contradiction of the opposite
sides of the wheel. The moon continues to be a
comfort.

I stand under the new moon, the dark moon and
whisper my wishes, my hopes and aspirations. I
allow myself to dream. The future is mine, I
know this. For I am cleansed and ready to
accept the new.

I give thanks to Grandmother moon. For the power. For the magic. For the love. For the lessons.

I follow the perpetual cycle, life is a journey, just the same as the moons journey around the Earth. Grandmother moon teaches us, all of us, no matter what phase we are in, we are always whole.

Mental Health

General Anxiety, OCD, PTSD, Health Anxiety, Eating Disorder and Depression can all look like this. Fine. Clever aren't we?

I'm not ashamed to say my mental health significantly deteriorated this last few years. Covid, work, family stress, my health - this year has been particularly bumpy and overwhelming. I've been let down and hurt. I've had a life changing diagnosis. I had some major alterations in my work life that didn't fit, that I didn't ask for or ever want.

I've also learnt how to deal with my mental health better in the last year than ever before. Self care, therapy, medication, howling at the moon, speaking up, taking time out, alternative and holistic therapies and concentrating on me.

My mental health isn't something I talk about. I deal with it with my smile and my mask on at all times. I'm smiley Sammy who is always available as the fixer of problems and the listener of others. The one who is always 'fine'.

And I know that makes me part of the problem - to suffer in silence.

And I'm not better, I'm not cured, but I'm working on it. And I'm one of the lucky ones. I am genuinely ok, I am coping mostly. This isn't pity.

So today, let's break that silence. Let's talk about mental health. Let's talk about who we are and how we cope. Let's also talk about the appalling lack of mental health services there are. The lack of integrity this government has in the face of the biggest health crisis of our time. Let's start the conversation and let's keep it going.

Reach out to your friends, talk about mental health, ask how people are, tell people how you really are. Normalise our mental health. Normalise therapy and medication. And if you're able to - Lobby your local MP. Join social media campaigns. Use your voice loudly if you can.

Be heard.

It's important. For you, for me, for them.

Lightness

I am calling in lightness. Lightness in the dark. Lightness in the dull. Lightness in the fear.

More happiness, more silliness, more fun, more ease.

Recognising that chink of light and working on expansion, not just hope that it's coming for me. Looking at life and wondering where I can make things easier, where I can stop the complications and glide right by negativity.

Avoiding the pseudo light which eventually brings you down. Splitting refracted light. Painting the light like a sticking plaster, over the darkness and issues.

Truly seeking and calling in the light, shining on the struggles and the hardships. Not reflecting, not dismissing. Just light.

Friendship

So very blessed that after 30 years, I have two women who are still my very best friends.

Life has given us all sorts of experiences, tragedy and elation. And we've been through it all together and emerged strong powerful women. Women who balance our lives like perpetual spinning plates, but still find time for each other and are always there when needed.

We are all three so different, but all three so similar and our lives are forever intrinsically intertwined. I'm so grateful to have them beside me every step of the way. So grateful to have held and have them hold me continually through life. So grateful to be part of something so special, it can't be described.

They have taught me more than they could ever know and support my growth in any way they can. We have our own personal cheerleaders in each other, I have my own personal support team in these beauties and I couldn't love them any more.

Having women around you, who truly support you, who lift you up, shelter you and speak the truth to you are the most valuable thing you'll ever find in life.

Wild

Can you hear the call of nature? Can you feel
the movement beneath your feet? Can you smell
the freedom, just beyond the summit?
You were once wild and free,
You were once untamed and free spirited, not in
a cage for all to see.

Shrunk, compliant, domesticated,
Unquestioning, small, observant,
It's just not for everyone.

Re-wilding is a real urge, re-wilding is a calling
like no other, re-wilding is felt within your
bones.

Growing yourself, healing your past,
remembering and honouring your ancestors,
Throwing off the expectations of todays society
and throwing compliance into the howling wind.

Re-wilding is not easy, not for the faint hearted.
But the possibilities are endless

Grief

Hold me close and go away
Please visit me and please don't stay
Talk to me but please don't speak
I need you NOW – come back next week.

Emotions muddled, needs unknown
To be with others or on my own?
To scream out loud? To rant and shout?
Or hide away and push you out?

I smile at you – "She's not that bad"
I shout at you – "She's going mad"
I speak to you – "What do I say?"
I show my tears – "Quick, walk away"

It's not catching, the grief I feel
I can't pretend that it's not real
I carry on as best I know
But this pain inside just won't go.

So true friends, please, accept the lot
I shout, I cry, I lose the plot
I don't know what I need today
So hold me close and go away.

Polarity

Life is funny isn't it.

A sad afternoon at a funeral and celebration of a young woman's life. A very vibrant young woman, survived by her 8 year old daughter and husband. Grief is just all encompassing, everywhere you look it's just the saddest time ever. The loss, the confusion, the guilt, the relief, the disbelief, the sadness and tears.

I pop into the shop on my way home and the young lad in there is celebrating his 21st birthday and has had the best weekend ever.

Such sadness and such happiness on the same day. Such a parallel universe between the two. Worlds apart.

It's hard to remember when you're going through the toughest time, that there ever was happiness.

Yet there is, right there. Happiness. Even if it's not yours. Someone somewhere is giving birth, getting married, celebrating a birthday, celebrating an achievement, gaining independence, many many reasons.

And it seems so wrong, so wrong that someone can be so happy, even though you are so sad. That in this case, the world has lost an amazing young woman - who has taught the world a thing or two and leaves a beautiful legacy behind. How does anyone have the right to be happy?

But it just goes to show doesn't it, life does indeed go on. Whether we like it or not. One persons darkest day is another's best day. Everyone's experiences and life journeys are so different, day to day, at all times. But it is just that, a journey. So be kind, whoever you meet and when, as you never know where on their journey they are and it could be incredibly different from yours.

So today, thank you for showing me those two extremes. I needed reminding there was still happiness in the world.

Good night, god bless young D and the happiest of birthdays to you, young sir xx

Stones

The gift of stones is always present. Stones in
my path, my shoe, my handbag - even my bed.

Stones gifted to me from the angels and
goddesses above.
Left for me by those gone by and held dearly.

Stones sent as a message, a reminder, a warning,
It's always stones.

For luck, for fortune, for gratitude.
Those stones line my path.

I see you

I see you.

Recovering with no support. No one else knowing what you consider your shame. Your beautiful friend - who you've now traumatised forever, but still sticks by you through thick and thin. I see you breaking your heart. Not talking about it, making it even more of a shameful secret. I see you questioning yourself.

I see you having flashbacks, suffering with your mental health - but attributing it to other parts of your painful story. I see you, losing your friends all over again, due to gossips, those you can't trust, those who stab you in the back, those who bully you.

I see you feeling the weight of people's judgements, even though they don't even know the truth. I see you trying to make things up to smooth over what you've been through and so no one finds out your truth.

I see you blaming yourself for all of it. I see you going a little crazy and behaving in ways you aren't proud of. No babe - this isn't how women behave to each other, but you're young, you'll learn that. #fuckthepatriarchy

I see you. And I see you are so so brave. I see you survive. You are 18. The last few years you've been through more than most adults have been through. I see your heartbreak. I see your shame. I see your need.

And I'm here to tell you - you survived. You are not to blame. You are a victim and a survivor. Things are complicated. You were a child. You can forgive. You can forgive those, you can forgive them.

You don't need any of these people who have wronged you. Because babe, at the grand old age of 39, you can finally cry about it all. About the tragedy, about the heartache and crying is truly releasing and with release - you can forgive. You'll learn how to do it proper with the full moon and everything.

And to be honest babe, you're going to grow in to your own skin, remember your family roots and heritage and grow up to be the witch your ancestors were desperate for you to be.

But you'll grow up to love women, to be a feminist, to know your worth, to know you are enough, to celebrate others, to empower others, to love your life, to join circles of like minded women and step into your power. You may even cry about this some more, when you bring it to the surface like this.

You deserved love. You deserve that hug. Better things are coming, I promise.

Busy

Must we always be busy? Must we always full every space and minute of our time? Must we only feel validated when we're racing around at a hundred miles an hour?
Is it society that makes it criminal to be slow? Is it the weight of other peoples expectations that ensures we never just stop. Even for one minute.
Learning to occupy yourself and rest, rather than use up every ounce of time and energy we have, is that such a bad thing?
Being present. Recognising the air around us. Appreciating the small things, the joy, the beauty, the breathe.
Racing around like headless chickens isn't conducive to a calm and gentle life.
We have to be busy at times, but it's important to contemplate the balance, it's important to know your worth. It's important once in a while, to stop.

Magic

Magic is in the air.

The wisdom of our ancestors, the whisper on the wind, the stones shining brightly gifted from Mother Earth.

The guidance from the Goddess, the fierceness of the storm, the lightness of the gifted feather which lands within your gaze.

The expanse of the ocean, the sounds of the forest, the knowing flicker of the flame in your ritual candle as it embodies your spell.

The love and laughter of your family, the support and well wishes of your friends, the grief and sadness we may all experience and share. The things that are always working out for us. The experiences that are never unmanageable. The helping hand in the dark.

Harnessing the magic, seeing the unexplained, knowing the Universe is listening. Tapping in to what you need, the salty sea air, the lushness of the ancient woods, the wisdom of the old crone.

The fairies, the devas, the Gods and Goddesses. The animals, the guides, the celestials and those gone before us. The crystals gifted to us from Gaia to teach us and remind us.

Your team. You.

Magic is all around us.

Milton Keynes UK
Ingram Content Group UK Ltd.
UKHW021051020524
442115UK00014B/463